Contents

Ham and bean chowder

Overall timing 2½ hours plus soaking

Freezing Not suitable

To serve 2

2 pints	Chicken stock	1.1 litres
4 oz	Dried haricot beans	125 g
2	Onions	2
1	Garlic clove	1
2	Stalks of celery	2
1 tbsp	Oil	15 ml
1	Medium ham hock	1
8 oz	Can of tomatoes	225 g
2	Cloves	2
1	Bay leaf	1
	Pepper	

Put stock and beans in a saucepan, bring to the boil and boil for 2 minutes. Remove from heat. Cover and leave to soak for 2 hours.

Peel and chop the onions; peel and crush garlic; chop celery. Heat the oil in a frying pan and fry onions, garlic and celery for about 5 minutes till soft but not brown. Add to saucepan with ham hock, tomatoes and their juice, cloves and bay leaf. Press tomatoes with a spoon to break them up.

Bring to the boil, then cover and simmer for 1½–2 hours till the ham is tender when pierced with a thin skewer.

Transfer ham hock to a plate and cool slightly. Remove the skin, fat and bones and discard. Cut the meat into cubes and set aside. Discard bay leaf and cloves.

Purée half the soup in a blender or vegetable mill. Return to rest of the soup and add the cubed ham. Simmer for 10 minutes, stirring occasionally. Adjust seasoning, then serve hot.

Cheese soup

Overall timing 35 minutes

Freezing Not suitable

To serve 2

3 oz	Gouda cheese	75 g
1½ oz	Butter	40 g
½ oz	Plain flour	15 g
1 pint	Stock	560 ml
	Salt and pepper	
4 tbsp	Single cream	4x15 ml
1	Egg yolk	1
1	Slice of bread	1
1 teasp	Oil	5 ml
1 teasp	Chopped parsley	5 ml
½ teasp	Chopped chives	2.5 ml
½ teasp	Chopped fresh dill	2.5 ml

Grate the cheese. Melt 1 oz (25 g) of the butter in a saucepan, stir in the flour and cook for 1 minute. Gradually stir in the stock and bring to the boil. Simmer for 10 minutes, stirring occasionally.

Stir cheese into pan and season with salt and pepper. Heat gently for a further 3 minutes till the cheese melts, but do not allow to boil.

Whisk the cream and egg yolk in a cup. Stir mixture into the soup and heat through without boiling.

Dice the bread. Melt remaining 1 oz (25 g) butter with the oil in a frying pan, add bread and fry till golden.

Place herbs in warmed soup bowls and pour in soup. Sprinkle croûtons on top.

Dutch vegetable soup

Overall timing 2¾ hours plus overnight soaking

Freezing Suitable: add cheese and cream after reheating

To serve 2

3 oz	Dried haricot beans	75 g
3 oz	Savoy cabbage	75 g
½	Onion	½
¼	Small cauliflower	¼
1	Leek	1
2 oz	Butter	50 g
	Salt and pepper	
1 oz	Edam cheese	25 g
2 teasp	Chopped parsley	2x5 ml
2 tbsp	Single cream	2x15 ml

Soak beans overnight in cold water. The next day, drain beans and cover with plenty of fresh cold water. Bring to the boil, cover and simmer for 1½–2 hours till tender.

Drain beans, reserving liquor. Purée beans in food mill or press through a sieve.

Shred cabbage. Peel and chop onion. Divide cauliflower into tiny florets. Trim and slice leek. Melt butter in saucepan, add prepared vegetables and fry for 10 minutes, stirring mixture frequently.

Add ¾ pint (400ml) reserved bean liquor, bean purée and seasoning. Cover and simmer for 15 minutes, stirring occasionally.

Grate cheese and stir into soup with chopped parsley and cream. Heat through gently for 5 minutes without boiling. Taste and adjust seasoning. Serve hot with fresh crusty bread.

Courgette and rice soup

Overall timing 1¼ hours

Freezing Suitable: reheat from frozen, then add cheese

To serve 2

1	Small onion	1
1 oz	Streaky bacon	25 g
1½ oz	Butter	40 g
4 oz	Courgettes	125 g
	Salt and pepper	
¾ pint	Chicken stock	400 ml
4 oz	Long grain rice	125 g
2 tbsp	Grated cheese	2x15 ml

Peel and chop onion; derind bacon and chop. Melt half the butter in a frying pan and fry onion and bacon gently till onion is soft.

Trim and dice courgettes. Add courgettes to pan and cook over a low heat until just tender. Season with salt and pepper.

Put stock in a large saucepan and bring to the boil. Add rice, cover and cook for 10 minutes. Add the courgette mixture and continue cooking till rice is tender.

Remove pan from heat and add remaining butter and the cheese. Stir well and serve at once.

Greek trout soup

Overall timing 1 hour

Freezing Not suitable

To serve 2

1 lb	Trout, cleaned	450 g
1	Stalk of celery	1
1	Large carrot	1
$\frac{1}{2}$	Small green pepper	$\frac{1}{2}$
2 tbsp	Olive oil	2x15 ml
3 oz	Long grain rice	75 g
1 pint	Water	560 ml
1	Egg	1
$1\frac{1}{2}$ tbsp	Lemon juice	22.5 ml
	Salt and pepper	

Cut the head and tail off trout and reserve. Cut the rest into 1 inch (2.5 cm) slices. Thinly slice the celery, with any leaves on. Peel and slice the carrot. Deseed and slice the pepper.

Heat the oil in a saucepan, add the prepared vegetables, cover and cook gently for 5 minutes.

Add the fish, including the head and tail, and the rice and fry for 5 minutes. Add the water and bring to the boil, stirring. Cover and simmer for 15–20 minutes till the rice is just tender.

Meanwhile, beat the egg lightly with a fork, then stir in the lemon juice. Remove fish head and tail from the soup with a draining spoon and discard. Add the egg mixture to the soup and stir over a low heat, without boiling, till the soup thickens slightly. Adjust the seasoning to taste and pour into two bowls. Serve with crusty bread and butter.

Leek and spinach soup

Overall timing 30 minutes

Freezing Not suitable

To serve 2

4 oz	Spinach	125 g
2	Leeks	2
1 oz	Butter	25 g
	Salt and pepper	
$\frac{3}{4}$ pint	Stock	400 ml
1 teasp	Lemon juice	5 ml
1 oz	Long grain rice	25 g
2 teasp	Grated Gruyère or Parmesan cheese	2 x 5 ml

Wash spinach thoroughly, removing any coarse stalks, and chop finely. Trim and thinly slice the leeks. Melt the butter in a saucepan. Add the spinach and leeks and seasoning. Cover and cook for 5 minutes.

Add stock and lemon juice and bring to the boil. Stir in the rice. Bring back to the boil and cook for 12–15 minutes or until the rice is tender. Taste and adjust seasoning.

Pour soup into two warmed soup bowls. Sprinkle the Gruyère or Parmesan cheese over the top and serve.

Goulash soup

Overall timing 1¼ hours

Freezing Suitable

To serve 2

1	Onion	1
1 oz	Lard	25 g
4 oz	Stewing beef	125 g
2 teasp	Plain flour	2x5 ml
1	Garlic clove	1
1 teasp	Hot or sweet paprika	5 ml
2 teasp	Tomato purée	2x5 ml
¾ pint	Beef stock	400 ml
	Grated rind of ¼ lemon	
	Salt and pepper	

Peel and finely chop the onion. Melt the lard in a saucepan and fry the onion for 5 minutes.

Cut the meat into small cubes. Toss in the flour and add to the pan with the peeled and crushed garlic and paprika. Fry, stirring, till meat is browned.

Stir in the tomato purée and gradually add the stock. Bring to the boil, stirring constantly. Cover and simmer for about 1 hour till the meat is tender.

Stir in the grated lemon rind and season to taste. Pour into warmed soup bowls and serve immediately with crusty bread.

Beer soup

Overall timing 25 minutes

Freezing Not suitable

To serve 2

2 teasp	Sugar	2x5 ml
½ pint	Milk	300 ml
	Strip of lemon rind	
	Pinch of ground cinnamon	
1 tbsp	Cornflour	15 ml
¼ pint	Beer	150 ml
1	Egg yolk	1
2 tbsp	Single cream	2x15 ml

Put the sugar, milk, lemon rind and cinnamon into a saucepan and heat through, stirring till sugar has dissolved. Blend cornflour with a little extra cold milk and add to the pan. Bring to the boil, stirring constantly. Cook for 3 minutes.

Put beer into another saucepan, heat through over a moderate heat, then stir into the milk mixture.

Lightly beat the egg yolk with the cream and whisk into the milk and beer. Cook, stirring, till thick and creamy but do not allow to boil. Discard lemon rind and serve soup with hot croûtons.

Variation

For a fruitier soup, replace the beer with still, dry cider. Just before serving, wash, core and thinly slice ½ small red-skinned apple and float slices on top.

Pork-stuffed mushrooms

Overall timing 40 minutes

Freezing Not suitable

To serve 2

4	Large cup mushrooms	4
½ oz	Fresh breadcrumbs	15 g
3 oz	Pork sausagemeat	75 g
1½ teasp	Chopped parsley	7.5 ml
2	Garlic cloves	2
	Pinch of cayenne	
	Salt	
½ oz	Butter	15 g
	Parsley sprigs	

Preheat the oven to 375°F (190°C) Gas 5.

Trim the mushrooms. Separate the stalks from the caps. Finely chop the mushroom stalks and place in a bowl. Add the breadcrumbs, sausagemeat, parsley, peeled and crushed garlic cloves, cayenne and salt. Mash with a fork till evenly mixed.

Spoon the mixture into the mushroom caps and arrange in a greased ovenproof dish. Dot with the butter and bake for 25 minutes.

Arrange on warmed serving dishes and garnish with parsley sprigs. Serve immediately with toast fingers.

Grapefruit with port

Overall timing 10 minutes plus chilling

Freezing Not suitable

To serve 2

1	**Large grapefruit**	1
2 tbsp	**Port**	2x15 ml

Cut the grapefruit in half. Cut round the flesh with a grapefruit knife. Divide into segments and remove membranes and pips.

Place the grapefruit halves on two serving plates and spoon 1 tbsp (15 ml) port over each. Chill for at least 30 minutes before serving.

Variation

Use medium or sweet sherry instead of port. If you like, the grapefruit may be grilled until lightly browned and served hot.

Tomatoes stuffed with buckling

Overall timing 40 minutes plus setting

Freezing Not suitable

To serve 2

1	Buckling	1
1½ tbsp	Thick mayonnaise	22.5 ml
2 teasp	Lemon juice	2x5 ml
	Salt	
1	Hard-boiled egg	1
1 teasp	Chopped parsley	5 ml
1 teasp	Chopped chives	5 ml
4 tbsp	Water	4x15 ml
	Pinch of sugar	
½ teasp	Vinegar	2.5 ml
2	Large tomatoes	2
2	Slices of Pumpernickel bread	2
	Butter	
	Lettuce leaves	
	Parsley	

Skin and bone the buckling. Chop flesh finely and place in a bowl. Add mayonnaise, lemon juice and salt. Shell and dice the hard-boiled egg and add with herbs to buckling mixture. Mix well.

Put water, sugar, pinch of salt and vinegar into a saucepan and heat till warm. Leave to cool, then add to buckling mixture.

Cut tops off tomatoes and remove the inside (this can be mixed into buckling mixture, if you like). Fill tomatoes with the buckling mixture and replace tops. Chill for 30 minutes.

Just before serving, put each tomato on to a slice of buttered Pumpernickel which should be slightly bigger than the base of the tomato. Serve on a bed of lettuce and garnish with parsley.

Cucumber and fruit salad

Overall timing 15 minutes

Freezing Not suitable

To serve 2

$\frac{1}{2}$	Cucumber	$\frac{1}{2}$
1	Orange	1
$\frac{1}{4}$	Honeydew melon	$\frac{1}{4}$
2 oz	Black grapes	50 g
	Sprigs of dill	
Dressing		
3 tbsp	Soured cream	3 x 15 ml
$1\frac{1}{2}$ teasp	Lemon juice	7.5 ml
1 tbsp	Caster sugar	15 ml
1 tbsp	Chopped fresh dill	15 ml
	Salt and pepper	

Thinly slice cucumber. Put into a bowl. Peel orange, remove pips and cut flesh into pieces. Peel melon, remove seeds and cut flesh into thin slices. Add orange and melon to cucumber with grapes. Chill for 20 minutes.

To make the dressing, beat soured cream, lemon juice, sugar, dill and seasoning in a bowl.

Divide salad between two serving glasses and spoon a little of the dressing over each. Garnish with dill sprigs and keep in refrigerator till ready to serve.

Celeriac cocktail

Overall timing 25 minutes

Freezing Not suitable

To serve 2

8 oz	Celeriac	225 g
	Salt	
1	Gherkin	1
1	Small tomato	1
1	Small banana	1
1	Small apple	1
3 fl oz	Plain yogurt	90 ml
2 teasp	Lemon juice	2x5 ml
	Sugar	
	Cayenne pepper	
	Lettuce leaves	

Peel and dice celeriac. Blanch in boiling salted water for 10 minutes, then drain and refresh under cold running water. Place in a bowl.

Chop gherkin and tomato; peel and chop banana; peel, core and chop apple. Put all in bowl with celeriac and mix well.

Mix together the yogurt, 1½ teasp (7.5 ml) lemon juice and a pinch each of salt, sugar and cayenne pepper.

Put a few lettuce leaves in each serving glass and sprinkle with remaining lemon juice. Divide salad between them, pour over dressing and garnish with parsley.

German kippers

Overall timing 30 minutes

Freezing Not suitable

To serve 2

2	Kipper fillets	2
1 teasp	Lemon juice	5 ml
1 teasp	Chopped parsley	5 ml
Sauce		
¼ pint	Plain yogurt	150 ml
1	Hard-boiled egg	1
	Tabasco sauce	
	Powdered mustard	
	Salt and pepper	
1	Tomato	1

Place kippers upright in a jug, pour in enough boiling water to cover and leave for 5 minutes. Drain kippers, dry on kitchen paper and cut into thin strips. Place in two serving glasses and sprinkle with lemon juice.

For the sauce, put the yogurt in a bowl. Shell and sieve the egg. Add to bowl with a few drops of Tabasco sauce, mustard to taste and seasoning. Mix well.

Blanch, peel and finely chop tomato. Add to sauce and mix gently. Spoon the sauce over the kippers, sprinkle with chopped parsley and serve with rye bread.

Piquant bananas

Jellied fruit cup

Overall timing 40 minutes including refrigeration

Freezing Not suitable

To serve 2

1	Shallot	1
1	Stalk of celery	1
4 tbsp	Tomato ketchup	4x15 ml
1 teasp	Worcestershire sauce	5 ml
2 tbsp	Lemon juice	2x15 ml
	Tabasco sauce	
2	Large bananas	2

Peel and finely chop the shallot. Chop the celery and put both into a bowl with the tomato ketchup, Worcestershire sauce and lemon juice. Mix well together and add a few drops of Tabasco sauce – how much will depend on individual preference.

Peel and slice bananas and add to mixture. Divide between two individual serving dishes and chill for 30 minutes before serving.

Overall timing 15 minutes plus chilling

Freezing Not suitable

To serve 2

1½ teasp	Powdered gelatine	7.5 ml
1 tbsp	Water	15 ml
5 oz	Canned mandarin oranges	150 g
4 oz	Canned pineapple chunks	125 g
2	Petits suisses cheeses	2
1 oz	Cocktail cherries	25 g
	Lettuce leaves	

Mix the gelatine with the water in a cup and leave till spongy.

Drain juice from mandarin oranges and pineapple. Place petits suisses in a bowl, add half juice gradually and beat well. Stir in oranges, pineapple and cherries.

Dissolve gelatine by placing cup in a pan of hot water. Stir into fruit mixture. Chill for 2 hours, then serve on bed of lettuce leaves in individual dishes.

Avocado and pine nut salad

Overall timing 15 minutes plus chilling

Freezing Not suitable

To serve 2

1	Large ripe avocado	1
1½ teasp	Lemon juice	7.5 ml
2	Gherkins	2
1 tbsp	Pine nuts	15 ml
1½ tbsp	Olive oil	22.5 ml
	Salt and pepper	
1	Garlic clove	1
4	Fresh mint leaves	4
2 tbsp	Plain yogurt	2x15 ml

Cut the avocado in half and remove the stone. Peel away the skin, dice the flesh and put into a bowl. Sprinkle with lemon juice and toss lightly till the avocado is coated.

Slice the gherkins thinly and add to the avocado with the pine nuts. Sprinkle with oil, season and toss.

Peel and crush the garlic into a small bowl. Wash the mint leaves and shred finely. Add to the garlic with the yogurt and mix well. Pour over the avocado and toss lightly. Chill for 1 hour.

Divide salad between two individual dishes and serve immediately with crusty rolls.

Italian deep-fried cheese

Overall timing 1¼ hours plus chilling

Freezing Not suitable

To serve 2

½	Onion	½
1 oz	Butter	25 g
2 oz	Long grain rice	50 g
4 fl oz	Chicken stock	120 ml
1 teasp	Grated Parmesan cheese	5 ml
	Pinch of grated nutmeg	
	Salt and pepper	
1 oz	Lean cooked ham	25 g
1½ oz	Mozzarella cheese	40 g
1	Egg	1
1 oz	Fine fresh breadcrumbs	25 g
	Oil for deep frying	

Peel and finely chop onion. Melt butter in a saucepan and fry onion till transparent.

Add rice and stir over a low heat for 2 minutes. Stir in stock, cover and bring to the boil. Simmer gently for 15–20 minutes till rice is tender. Remove from heat and stir in Parmesan, nutmeg and seasoning. Leave to cool completely.

Meanwhile, chop ham finely. Cut Mozzarella into four sticks about 1½ inches (4 cm) long and ½ inch (12.5 mm) thick. Break egg on to a plate and beat lightly with a fork. Spread breadcrumbs on another plate.

Beat a little egg and the ham into rice. Put 2 tbsp (2x15 ml) rice mixture in palm of one hand. Place a cheese stick on top and cover with more rice. Pat into a cylinder shape about 2½ inches (6.5 cm) long and 1 inch (2.5 cm) thick. Brush beaten egg over croquette, then coat with breadcrumbs. Shape and coat three more croquettes. Chill for 1 hour.

Heat oil in a deep-fryer to 360°F (180°C). Fry the croquettes for 5–6 minutes till golden. Drain on kitchen paper and serve hot.

Camembert fish bake

Overall timing 45 minutes

Freezing Not suitable

To serve 2

2	White fish fillets	2
1 teasp	Lemon juice	5 ml
3–4	Large ripe tomatoes	3–4
4 oz	Camembert cheese	125 g
	Salt and pepper	
2 tbsp	Fresh breadcrumbs	2x15 ml
1½ teasp	Chopped parsley	7.5 ml
5 tbsp	Single cream	5x15 ml
½ oz	Butter	15 g

Preheat the oven to 400°F (200°C) Gas 6. Remove skin from fish fillets and halve them. Place two halves in greased ovenproof dish and sprinkle with half the lemon juice.

Blanch, peel and slice the tomatoes. Cut the Camembert into very thin slices. Arrange half the cheese, then the tomatoes, then remaining cheese over the fish and season. Cover with remaining fish and lemon juice.

Sprinkle the breadcrumbs and parsley over the fish and pour the cream over. Season and dot with butter.

Bake for 25 minutes till the fish is tender. Serve hot with sauté potatoes and a tomato and onion salad.

Trout with almonds

Overall timing 20 minutes

Freezing Not suitable

To serve 2

2	Trout, cleaned	2
1 oz	Plain flour	25 g
2 oz	Butter	50 g
2 tbsp	Chopped parsley	2x15 ml
2 oz	Flaked almonds	50 g
	Salt and pepper	
2	Lemon slices	2

Dust trout with flour. Melt butter in frying pan. Add trout and cook gently on one side for 5 minutes.

Turn trout over with a fish slice. Add half the parsley, the almonds and seasoning. Cook for a further 7–8 minutes till fish is tender and almonds are golden brown (turn them as they cook).

Place fish on warmed serving plates and spoon over almonds. Garnish with lemon slices and remaining chopped parsley. Serve with boiled potatoes and a mixed salad.

Welsh trout

Overall timing 45 minutes

Freezing Not suitable

To serve 2

1 teasp	Chopped fresh sage	5 ml
1 teasp	Chopped fresh rosemary	5 ml
1 teasp	Chopped fresh thyme	5 ml
1 tbsp	Chopped parsley	15 ml
	Salt and pepper	
2 oz	Butter	50 g
2x1 lb	Trout, cleaned	2x450 g
4	Streaky bacon rashers	4

Preheat the oven to 350°F (180°C) Gas 4.

Beat the herbs and seasoning into the butter and spread half inside each fish. Derind and stretch the bacon. Wrap two rashers around each fish, securing with wooden cocktail sticks.

Place the trout in a greased ovenproof dish, cover with foil and bake for about 25 minutes till tender.

Remove the cocktail sticks, place the trout on a warmed serving dish and garnish with lemon slices and sprigs of parsley. Surround with lettuce leaves, mustard and cress and tomato wedges and serve immediately.

Whiting curls

Overall timing 50 minutes

Freezing Not suitable

To serve 2

2	Small whiting	2
	Salt and pepper	
4 tbsp	Plain flour	4x15 ml
	Oil for deep frying	
1	Lemon	1
	Sprigs of parsley	

Scale and dry the whiting. Place one on its side on a board and hold it firmly by the tail. Using a sharp knife in a sawing action cut between the flesh and the back-bone to just behind the head.

Turn the fish over and repeat the action on the other side to expose the backbone. Cut off the backbone just behind the head with kitchen scissors. Repeat with the other whiting.

Curl fish, pushing tail through skin at far side of mouth to hold in place. Lightly coat each fish with seasoned flour. Shake off any excess.

Heat the oil in a deep-fryer to 340°F (170°C). Fry the whiting for about 10 minutes till tender and golden brown. Drain on kitchen paper and arrange the fish on a warmed serving dish. Garnish with parsley and lemon and serve immediately, with tartare sauce.

Bream with mushrooms

Overall timing 1 hour

Freezing Not suitable

To serve 2

2 lb	Bream or other whole fish	900 g
4 oz	Button mushrooms	125 g
1	Small onion	1
	Salt and pepper	
4 fl oz	Water	120 ml
1 teasp	Chopped parsley	5 ml
	Pinch of dried thyme	
1 oz	Butter	25 g
1	Lemon	1

Preheat the oven to 400°F (200°C) Gas 6.

Clean fish, but don't remove head. Trim tail and fins, and wash well. Dry on kitchen paper.

Thinly slice button mushrooms. Peel and finely chop onion. Cover bottom of ovenproof dish with most of mushrooms and onion and place the fish on top. Season with salt and pepper, and pour in the water. Sprinkle fish with parsley, thyme and remaining mushrooms and onion.

Melt butter and pour over fish. Cover dish with foil or a lid and bake for 40 minutes, basting frequently with juices in dish. Turn fish over halfway through cooking time and remove foil for last 10 minutes. The fish is cooked when the flesh becomes opaque.

Garnish with lemon and serve with boiled new potatoes.

Curried cockles with rice

Overall timing 30 minutes

Freezing Not suitable

To serve 2

4 oz	Long grain rice	125 g
	Salt	
1 lb	Cockles	450 g
Curry sauce		
1	Small onion	1
1	Garlic clove	1
1 oz	Butter	25 g
1 tbsp	Curry powder	15 ml
	Ground cinnamon	
	Ground ginger	
	Sugar	
4 tbsp	Boiling water	4x15 ml
	Salt and pepper	

Cook the rice in boiling salted water till tender.

Meanwhile, scrub the cockles well under cold running water. Place them in a saucepan of salted water. Bring to the boil, cover and cook gently till the shells open. Discard any that do not open. Remove cockles from their shells and set aside. Strain the cooking liquor through a muslin-lined sieve into bowl.

Peel and finely chop onion and garlic. Melt butter in a frying pan and fry the onion and garlic till transparent. Add the curry powder and cook for a further 2 minutes. Add a large pinch each of cinnamon, ginger and sugar and the boiling water. Add 5 tbsp (5x15 ml) of the cooking liquor from the cockles. Taste, and season if necessary.

Stir the cockles into the sauce and heat through quickly. Put the drained rice on a warmed serving dish and pour the cockles and sauce over. Serve hot.

Skate with capers

Overall timing 25 minutes

Freezing Not suitable

To serve 2

2x8 oz	Pieces of skate	2x225 g
	Salt and pepper	
1½ teasp	Vinegar	7.5 ml
1½ oz	Butter	40 g
1 tbsp	Capers	15 ml
1 tbsp	Chopped parsley	15 ml
1½ tbsp	Lemon juice	22.5 ml
2 tbsp	Single cream	2x15 ml

Put the skate into a saucepan. Cover with cold water and add a little salt and a few drops of vinegar. Bring to the boil, then remove from the heat, cover and leave to stand for 10 minutes.

Drain and dry the skate; remove the skin. Place on a warmed serving dish and keep hot.

Melt the butter in a small saucepan and stir in remaining vinegar, the capers, parsley, lemon juice, cream and seasoning. Cook for 2–3 minutes, without boiling, till heated through. Pour over the skate. Serve with boiled or steamed potatoes and a tossed green salad.

Grilled cod with bacon

Overall timing 25 minutes

Freezing Not suitable

To serve 2

2	Large cod fillets	2
2 tbsp	Oil	2x15 ml
	Salt and pepper	
2 oz	Thin streaky bacon rashers	50 g
1 oz	Butter	25 g
1 tbsp	Lemon juice	15 ml
	Sprigs of parsley	
	Lemon wedges	

Preheat the grill.

Brush the cod fillets with oil and season with salt and pepper. Place under a fairly hot grill and cook for about 15 minutes, turning fillets over halfway through cooking time.

Remove rind from the bacon, then grill or fry. Drain on kitchen paper.

Melt the butter in a small saucepan, taking care not to colour it. Arrange the fish and bacon on warmed serving plates. Pour the butter over and sprinkle with lemon juice. Garnish with parsley sprigs and lemon wedges. Serve with boiled potatoes tossed in butter and sprinkled with chopped parsley, and a crisp lettuce salad.

Barbecued haddock

Overall timing 20 minutes plus marination

Freezing Not suitable

To serve 2

1½ tbsp	Oil	22.5 ml
1½ teasp	Lemon juice	7.5 ml
1 tbsp	Soft brown sugar	15 ml
¼ teasp	Chilli powder	1.25 ml
½ teasp	Worcestershire sauce	2.5 ml
1 teasp	Tomato purée	5 ml
1 lb	Smoked haddock	450 g

Mix together oil, lemon juice, sugar, chilli powder, Worcestershire sauce and tomato purée in a shallow dish. Add the haddock, cover and marinate in the refrigerator for 1 hour, turning fish once or twice.

Preheat the grill.

Remove fish from marinade and place on a large piece of foil on the grill pan. Grill for 5–7 minutes on each side, brushing with marinade from time to time.

Alternatively, place the fish in a fish holder and barbecue over charcoal.

Baked perch with herbs

Overall timing 35 minutes

Freezing Not suitable

To serve 2

2x1 lb	Perch or similar fish	2x450 g
	Salt and pepper	
2	Bay leaves	2
2	Sage leaves	2
2	Sprigs of rosemary	2
2 oz	Butter	50 g
2 tbsp	Chopped parsley	2x15 ml
2 tbsp	Lemon juice	2x15 ml
2 tbsp	Olive oil	2x15 ml
	Lemon slices	

Preheat the oven to 425°F (220°C) Gas 7.

Clean and scale the fish, then wash and dry. Sprinkle inside and out with salt and pepper and put a bay leaf, a sage leaf and a sprig of rosemary inside each with $\frac{1}{2}$ oz (15 g) of butter.

Grease sheet of foil with the remaining butter and put into a roasting tin. Place the fish in the centre, sprinkle with the parsley and pour the lemon juice and oil over. Wrap the foil around the fish and seal the edges together well. Bake for about 20 minutes till tender.

Lift the fish out of the foil and place on a warmed serving dish. Pour the cooking liquor over and garnish with fresh herbs and the lemon slices. Serve with creamed potatoes and baked tomatoes.

Variation

For a more substantial filling, bind 4 oz (125 g) fresh breadcrumbs, chopped herbs, grated lemon rind and seasoning with 1 egg, fill fish and bake for 25 minutes.

Steak and onions

Overall timing 30 minutes

Freezing Not suitable

To serve 2

12 oz	Medium onions	350 g
3 oz	Butter	75 g
1 tbsp	Oil	15 ml
2	Porterhouse steaks	2
5 tbsp	White wine	5x15 ml
	Pinch of sugar	
	Salt and pepper	

Peel and slice the onions into rings. Melt 1 oz (25 g) of the butter with the oil in a frying pan and fry the onions, stirring frequently, till brown and tender.

Meanwhile, melt the remaining butter in another frying pan and fry the steaks for about 4 minutes on each side, according to taste. Place the steaks on a warmed serving plate and keep hot.

Add the steak cooking juices to the onions with the wine, sugar and seasoning. Stir well, then cook over high heat till the liquid reduces by about half. Pour over the steaks and serve, with boiled new potatoes.

Hamburgers with eggs

Overall timing 10 minutes

Freezing Not suitable

To serve 2

2	Onions	2
8 oz	Finely minced beef	225 g
	Salt and pepper	
2 teasp	Oil	2x5 ml
2	Tomatoes	2
2 oz	Butter	50 g
2	Eggs	2
	Cayenne	
	Watercress	

Peel the onions. Finely chop half of one and cut the other half and the second onion into rings. Mix the chopped onion with the beef and season. Divide in half and shape into burgers.

Heat the oil in a frying pan and fry the burgers for about 5 minutes on each side. Add the tomatoes halfway through the cooking.

Meanwhile, melt 1 oz (25 g) butter in another frying pan and fry the onion rings till crisp. Remove from the pan and keep hot.

Add the eggs to the pan with the remaining butter and fry till set.

Top each burger with an egg and arrange on warmed plates with the onions and tomatoes. Sprinkle a little cayenne over the eggs. Keep hot.

Put the watercress into the pan with the butter and fry quickly. Use to garnish the burgers.

Veal parcels

Overall timing 40 minutes

Freezing Not suitable

To serve 2

2 oz	Butter	50 g
1½ teasp	Plain flour	7.5 ml
¼ pint	Milk	150 ml
	Salt and pepper	
1 oz	Gruyère cheese	25 g
1 tbsp	Oil	15 ml
8 oz	Veal escalope	225 g
2	Slices of cooked ham	2

Melt 1 oz (25 g) of the butter in a saucepan. Stir in the flour and cook over low heat for 2–3 minutes. Gradually add the milk. Bring to the boil, stirring till thickened. Season. Remove from the heat and stir in the grated cheese.

Preheat the oven to 425°F (220°C) Gas 7.

Melt remaining butter with the oil in a frying pan. Add escalope and cook on each side for 4 minutes. Season, then cut in half.

Cut two large heart shapes out of grease-proof paper and grease the edges. In the centre of each heart place a slice of ham, then half an escalope and a good layer of sauce. Fold ham over the filling.

Close parcels securely and place on baking tray. Bake for 15 minutes, then serve hot.

Veal chops with herbs

Overall timing 45 minutes

Freezing Not suitable

To serve 2

2	Veal chops	2
	Salt and pepper	
1 tbsp	Plain flour	15 ml
½ oz	Butter	15 g
1 tbsp	Oil	15 ml
5 tbsp	Dry white wine	5x15 ml
1 tbsp	Chopped parsley	15 ml
1 tbsp	Chopped fresh chervil	15 ml
1 tbsp	Chopped fresh tarragon	15 ml
5 tbsp	Chicken stock	5x15 ml
Garnish		
	Sprigs of chervil or parsley	
1	Tomato	1

Season chops on both sides, then coat with flour. Heat the butter and oil in a frying pan and cook chops for 15 minutes on each side. Remove chops from pan and keep warm.

Add wine and herbs to pan juices and stir well. Bring to the boil and add stock. Cook for 10 minutes, then return chops to pan and cook for 2–3 minutes more.

Garnish with chervil or parsley and tomato quarters and serve with boiled potatoes, carrots and peas.

Pork chops with wine sauce

Overall timing 30 minutes

Freezing Not suitable

To serve 2

1 oz	Butter	25 g
2	Pork chops	2
	Salt and pepper	
1	Small onion	1
3 tbsp	Dry white wine	3x15 ml
3 tbsp	Water	3x15 ml
1½ teasp	Tomato purée	7.5 ml
4	Gherkins	4
1 teasp	Chopped parsley	5 ml
½ teasp	Made mustard	2.5 ml

Melt the butter in the frying pan and cook the pork chops gently for 10–12 minutes on each side. Season. Place on warmed serving dish and keep warm.

Peel and finely chop onion. Add to pan and fry till transparent. Stir in wine, water, tomato purée and seasoning and bring to the boil, stirring. Simmer for 3 minutes.

Remove pan from heat. Thinly slice two of the gherkins and stir into the sauce with the parsley and mustard. Pour sauce over chops. Garnish with remaining gherkins, cut into fan shapes, and serve with macaroni or noodles.

Sausage and potato salad

Overall timing 25 minutes

Freezing Not suitable

To serve 2

12 oz	Medium-size new potatoes	350 g
	Salt and pepper	
1 tbsp	Dry white wine	15 ml
4–6 oz	German spicy sausage	125–175 g
1½ teasp	Chopped parsley	7.5 ml
½ teasp	Made mustard	2.5 ml
2 tbsp	Oil	2x15 ml
1½ teasp	Vinegar	7.5 ml
	Sprigs of parsley	

Scrub the potatoes, put into a saucepan, cover with cold salted water and bring to the boil. Simmer for about 15 minutes till tender. Drain and peel, then slice thickly and put into a serving dish. Sprinkle with the white wine.

Remove outer covering from the sausage and slice thickly. Add to the potatoes with the chopped parsley.

Mix the mustard, oil, pepper and vinegar together and pour over the salad. Toss gently. Garnish with sprigs of parsley and serve warm or cold.

Russian lamb burgers

Overall timing 30 minutes

Freezing Suitable: coat with flour and fry after thawing

To serve 2

1 oz	Fresh breadcrumbs	25 g
2 tbsp	Milk	2x15 ml
8 oz	Minced shoulder of lamb	225 g
1 oz	Gruyère cheese	25 g
1	Small egg	1
	Salt and pepper	
1 tbsp	Plain flour	15 ml
1 oz	Butter	25 g
8 oz	Can of tomatoes	226 g

Put breadcrumbs in a large bowl with the milk and soak for a few minutes. Add the lamb, grated cheese, egg and seasoning and mix well. Divide the mixture into four and shape into patties. Coat lightly with flour.

Melt butter in a frying pan and fry for 5 minutes on each side. Remove from pan with a spatula and place on a warmed serving dish. Keep hot.

Heat tomatoes in a saucepan. Drain and arrange on serving dish with the burgers. Serve a hot tomato sauce separately, if liked, and mashed potatoes topped with crisp fried breadcrumbs and bacon bits.

Lamb curry

Overall timing 1½ hours

Freezing Suitable

To serve 2

1 lb	Boned lamb	450 g
1	Onion	1
1 oz	Butter	25 g
1 tbsp	Oil	15 ml
1 teasp	Curry powder	5 ml
	Salt and pepper	
1½ tbsp	Plain flour	22.5 ml
8 fl oz	Stock	220 ml
½ teasp	Tomato purée	2.5 ml
	Bouquet garni	
1	Tomato	1
½	Green pepper	½
2 oz	Button mushrooms	50 g
6 oz	New potatoes	175 g

Cut meat into cubes. Peel and chop onion. Heat butter and oil in a frying pan and fry onion till transparent.

Add curry powder and cook, stirring, for 2 minutes. Add meat and cook till golden on all sides. Season with salt and pepper, sprinkle with flour and stir over a high heat for a few minutes.

Reduce heat and stir in stock and tomato purée. Add bouquet garni and bring to the boil, stirring. Cover and cook gently for 40 minutes, stirring occasionally.

Chop tomato; deseed and slice pepper; halve or slice larger mushrooms. Scrub potatoes but don't peel; cut into chunks.

Add prepared vegetables to pan and cook for a further 20 minutes. Discard bouquet garni before serving, with plain boiled rice.

Kidneys in mustard sauce

Overall timing 20 minutes

Freezing Not suitable

To serve 2

8 oz	Lamb's kidneys	225 g
	Salt and pepper	
2 oz	Butter	50 g
5 tbsp	Dry white wine	5x15 ml
1 tbsp	Lemon juice	15 ml
1 teasp	French mustard	5 ml

Prepare and halve kidneys. Season well. Melt 1 oz (25 g) butter in a frying pan, add kidney halves and cook for 5 minutes on each side until golden. Remove from pan, arrange on warmed serving plate and keep hot.

Add wine to pan and cook for 2–3 minutes. Blend lemon juice and mustard and stir into pan with remaining butter and seasoning. Heat through, stirring, but do not boil.

Pour sauce over kidneys and serve immediately with boiled cauliflower and buttered green beans.

Chicken with pineapple

Overall timing 45 minutes

Freezing Not suitable

To serve 2

1½ lb	Chicken joints	675 g
2 teasp	Potato flour or cornflour	2x5 ml
3 tbsp	Oil	3x15 ml
1 tbsp	Soy sauce	15 ml
1½ teasp	Dry sherry	7.5 ml
	Salt and pepper	
4 oz	Canned pineapple rings or chunks	125 g

Remove meat from chicken joints and cut it into chunky pieces.

Mix together potato flour or cornflour, half the oil, the soy sauce, sherry and seasoning in a bowl. Add the chicken pieces and coat well. Leave to marinate for 15 minutes.

Heat the rest of the oil in a heavy-based saucepan. Drain the chicken, saving the marinade, and add to the pan. Cook over a fairly high heat for 5 minutes, stirring constantly.

Drain the pineapple, reserving 4 tbsp (4x15 ml) of the syrup. Cut the rings into sections or halve the chunks. Add the reserved marinade from the chicken and the pineapple pieces to the pan and cook for a further 12 minutes, continually turning the chicken over.

When the chicken is golden brown, add the reserved pineapple syrup, adjust seasoning and cook for a further 5 minutes. Serve with saffron rice.

Chicken in a basket

Overall timing 40 minutes

Freezing Not suitable

To serve 2

2x1 lb	Ovenready poussins	2x450 g
2 tbsp	Oil	2x15 ml
	Salt and pepper	
1 lb	Potatoes	450 g
	Oil for frying	
	Fresh parsley	
1	Small onion	1

Preheat the oven to 400°F (200°C) Gas 6.

Place the poussins in roasting tin. Brush with oil and season well. Roast for 30 minutes, or until juices from the legs run clear when pierced with a skewer.

Meanwhile, peel potatoes and cut into thin, matchstick chips. Heat oil in a deep-fryer to 340°F (170°C). Fry chips for 3–5 minutes till golden. Drain well.

Arrange napkins in two small baskets. Place chips in folds of cloth. Place poussins in baskets. Garnish with parsley sprigs and onion rings. Eat with your fingers or a knife and fork if preferred.

Variation

To make barbecue-style poussins, mix together 2 tbsp (2x15 ml) tomato purée, 1 tbsp (15 ml) Worcestershire sauce, 1 tbsp (15 ml) oil, 1 peeled and crushed garlic clove and seasoning. Spread over poussins, cover with foil and roast for 40 minutes. Serve as above.

Roast pigeons with mushrooms

Overall timing 50 minutes

Freezing Not suitable

To serve 2

4 oz	Small onions	125 g
2	Small ovenready pigeons	2
2	Sprigs of rosemary	2
4	Sage leaves	4
3 oz	Streaky bacon rashers	75 g
3 oz	Butter	75 g
4 oz	Mushrooms	125 g
5 tbsp	Dry white wine	5 x 15 ml
	Salt and pepper	

Preheat the oven to 450°F (230°C) Gas 8.

Blanch the onions in boiling water for 5 minutes, then peel. Wipe the pigeons and put a sprig of rosemary, two sage leaves and a rasher of bacon into each. Put into a roasting tin and spread half the butter over. Roast for about 15 minutes till browned.

Meanwhile, derind and chop the remaining bacon. Melt the remaining butter in a flame-proof casserole and fry the onions and bacon till just golden. Thickly slice the mushrooms. Add to onions and bacon and fry for 2 minutes.

Remove the pigeons from the oven and reduce the temperature to 400°F (200°C) Gas 6. Put the pigeons into the casserole on top of the vegetables, pour the wine over and season.

Cover the casserole, place in the oven and cook for a further 15–20 minutes till the pigeons are tender. Adjust the seasoning before serving.

Braised pork chops

Overall timing 55 minutes

Freezing Not suitable

To serve 2

4	Pork chops	4
	Salt and pepper	
2	Cooking apples	2
2	Onions	2
1 oz	Butter	25 g
3 fl oz	Water	90 ml
2 teasp	Worcestershire sauce	2x5 ml
	Fresh parsley	

Season chops with salt and pepper. Peel and core apples and cut into wedges. Peel onions and cut into rings.

Melt butter in frying pan and brown the chops on all sides. Add water and Worcestershire sauce, cover and cook for 10 minutes.

Turn chops over. Add apples and onions. Reduce heat, cover and cook for a further 30 minutes.

Garnish with parsley and serve with creamed potatoes.

Sweetbread bake

Overall timing 50 minutes

Freezing Not suitable

To serve 2

2 oz	Button mushrooms	50 g
8 oz	Prepared lambs' sweetbreads	225 g
	Salt and pepper	
2 tbsp	Plain flour	2x15 ml
1 oz	Butter	25 g
5 tbsp	Chicken stock	5x15 ml
1	Small egg	1
5 tbsp	Plain yogurt	5x15 ml
2 oz	Cheese	50 g
	Chopped parsley	

Preheat the oven to 375°F (190°C) Gas 5.

Slice the mushrooms. Cut the sweetbreads into $\frac{1}{4}$ inch (6 mm) thick slices. Season the flour and toss the sweetbreads in it till lightly coated.

Melt butter in a frying pan, add the sweetbreads and mushrooms and fry for about 10 minutes till golden. Add the stock and seasoning and simmer for 5 minutes.

Meanwhile, beat the egg with yogurt, grated cheese and seasoning.

Arrange the sweetbreads and mushrooms in an ovenproof dish and pour the yogurt mixture over. Bake for 20 minutes till lightly set and golden. Sprinkle with parsley and serve hot.

Chicken in foil

Overall timing 1 hour

Freezing Not suitable

To serve 2

2	Boned chicken or turkey breasts	2
	Salt and pepper	
1 tbsp	Plain flour	15 ml
2 oz	Butter	50 g
2	Sage leaves	2
1 tbsp	Brandy	15 ml
4 fl oz	Chicken stock	120 ml
4 oz	Chicken livers	125 g
2 oz	Mushrooms	50 g
1 oz	Cooked ham	25 g

Coat chicken or turkey breasts with seasoned flour. Melt half butter in a frying pan and fry chicken or turkey breasts on each side till golden. Add sage, brandy and stock and bring to boil. Cover and simmer for 15 minutes.

Preheat the oven to 400°F (200°C) Gas 6.

Finely chop chicken livers, mushrooms and ham. Melt remaining butter in another frying pan and stir-fry liver, mushrooms and ham for 5 minutes. Remove from heat.

Cut two large foil rectangles and put a chicken or turkey breast in centre of each. Spread liver mixture on top and spoon over pan juices. Wrap foil round to make secure parcels, then place in roasting tin. Bake for 20 minutes.

Stuffed turkey rolls

Overall timing 1¼ hours

Freezing Not suitable

To serve 2

1	Small onion	1
1	Garlic clove	1
2 oz	Butter	50 g
1	Large tomato	1
	Salt and pepper	
1 oz	Fresh breadcrumbs	25 g
1½ teasp	Chopped parsley	7.5 ml
½	Egg	½
2x6 oz	Turkey escalopes	2x175 g
2	Bacon rashers	2
5 tbsp	Dry white wine	5x15 ml
1 teasp	Lemon juice	5 ml

Peel and finely chop onion and garlic. Melt half butter in a saucepan and fry onion till golden.

Blanch, peel and chop tomato and add to pan with garlic and seasoning. Simmer till thick. Remove from heat; add crumbs, parsley and egg.

Season escalopes. Divide stuffing between them and roll up. Wrap a bacon rasher round each roll and secure with wooden cocktail sticks.

Melt remaining butter in frying pan and fry rolls till browned all over. Add wine and lemon juice, cover and simmer for 20 minutes.

Lamb-stuffed courgettes

Overall timing 1½ hours

Freezing Suitable: bake from frozen, covered, in 350°F (180°C) Gas 4 oven for about 45 minutes

To serve 2

1 oz	Long grain rice	25 g
	Salt and pepper	
1	Large onion	1
1 tbsp	Oil	15 ml
4 oz	Minced lamb	125 g
2–4	Courgettes	2–4
2	Tomatoes	2
1	Garlic clove	1
2 oz	Petits pois	50 g
¼ pint	Stock	150 ml
4 oz	Emmenthal cheese	125 g
1 oz	Butter	25 g

Preheat the oven to 350°F (180°C) Gas 4.

Cook rice in boiling salted water for 10–12 minutes till just tender.

Meanwhile, peel and finely chop onion. Heat oil in a frying pan and fry onion till transparent. Add minced lamb and fry till brown, stirring all the time. Season well with salt and pepper.

Trim courgettes and halve them lengthways. Scoop out most of the flesh with melon baller or small spoon. Sprinkle courgette shells with a little salt. Chop scooped out flesh and add to lamb mixture.

Blanch, peel and finely chop tomatoes. Peel and crush garlic. Add tomatoes and garlic to lamb with peas, drained rice and seasoning. Mix well.

Fill courgette shells with mixture. Place side by side in dish, pour round stock, cover and bake for 25 minutes.

Sprinkle with grated cheese and dot with butter. Bake, uncovered, for a further 10 minutes.

Black pudding with apples

Overall timing 25 minutes

Freezing Not suitable

To serve 2

8 oz	Black pudding	225 g
2 oz	Butter	50 g
1	Onion	1
2	Dessert apples	2
	Fresh parsley	

Thickly slice the black pudding. Melt the butter in a frying pan and add the black pudding. Cook till crispy – if you cook them gently the slices will stay intact, instead of breaking away from the skin. Lift out with draining spoon and keep hot.

Peel onion and slice into rings. Fry gently in the butter till brown and just tender.

Core and slice the apples. Add to pan and cook for 5 minutes, turning slices over half-way. Add the pudding and cook the mixture for 2 minutes more.

Place black pudding, onion and apples on two warmed plates. Garnish with parsley sprigs and serve hot.

Piquant kidneys

Overall timing 30 minutes

Freezing Not suitable

To serve 2

8 oz	Lamb's kidneys	225 g
2	Streaky bacon rashers	2
1	Onion	1
8 oz	Long macaroni	225 g
	Salt and pepper	
1 oz	Butter	25 g
1½ teasp	Plain flour	7.5 ml
½ pint	Beef stock	300 ml
1½ teasp	Tomato purée	7.5 ml
¼ teasp	Dried sage	1.25 ml

Prepare and thinly slice kidneys. Derind and dice bacon. Peel and chop onion. Cook macaroni in boiling salted water for 15 minutes till tender.

Meanwhile, melt butter in frying pan and fry kidneys for 3 minutes, stirring from time to time. Remove from pan.

Add bacon and onion to pan and fry gently till golden. Sprinkle flour over and cook, stirring, for 2 minutes. Add stock, tomato purée, sage and seasoning. Bring to the boil, stirring, then return kidneys to pan, reduce heat and simmer for 15 minutes.

Drain macaroni and arrange in warmed serving dish. Spoon kidneys and sauce over and serve hot with crisp lettuce and cucumber salad.

Olive and caper pizza

Overall timing 1¾ hours

Freezing Not suitable

To serve 2

6 oz	Potatoes	175 g
	Salt and pepper	
8 oz	Self-raising flour	225 g
2 oz	Butter	50 g
12 oz	Tomatoes	350 g
4	Anchovy fillets	4
1 tbsp	Capers	15 ml
4 oz	Black olives	125 g
4 tbsp	Milk	4x15 ml
2 teasp	Dried oregano	2x5 ml
1 tbsp	Olive oil	15 ml

Preheat the oven to 425°F (220°C) Gas 7.

Peel potatoes and cut into small chunks. Cook in boiling salted water till tender.

Meanwhile, sift the flour into a bowl and rub in the butter till the mixture resembles fine breadcrumbs. Blanch, peel and chop tomatoes. Chop anchovy fillets. Drain capers. Stone olives.

Drain potatoes and mash well. Stir into rubbed-in mixture. Add milk and mix to form a soft dough. Knead lightly till smooth. Roll out dough and use to line a greased 9 inch (23 cm) pizza pan or flan tin.

Arrange tomatoes, anchovies, capers and olives on top. Sprinkle with salt, pepper and oregano. Sprinkle olive oil over and bake for about 55 minutes till well risen and golden. Cut into wedges to serve.

Cheesy fish croquettes

Overall timing 40 minutes

Freezing Suitable: reheat from frozen in 375°F (190°C) Gas 5 oven for 30 minutes

To serve 2

8 oz	White fish fillets	225 g
½ pint	Milk	300 ml
1	Small onion	1
2 oz	Butter	50 g
2 oz	Plain flour	50 g
1	Hard-boiled egg	1
1 tbsp	Grated Parmesan cheese	15 ml
	Salt and pepper	
	Oil for frying	

Place the fish fillets in a large frying pan with the milk. Cover and cook over a moderate heat for about 10 minutes till fish is tender. Lift fish out of milk. Discard skin and any bones, then mash flesh. Reserve fish and milk.

Peel and finely chop the onion. Melt the butter in clean frying pan and fry onion till transparent. Add the flour and cook for 2 minutes, stirring. Gradually stir in the reserved milk and bring to the boil.

Remove pan from heat and add the reserved fish. Shell and finely chop the hard-boiled egg and add to the sauce with the Parmesan and seasoning. Spread the mixture thickly on to a plate, cover and chill till firm.

Divide the mixture into four and shape on a well floured board into round patties about ½ inch (12.5 mm) thick.

Heat oil in deep-fryer to 340°F (170°C) and fry the croquettes for 5 minutes till crisp and golden. Drain on kitchen paper and serve hot.

Anchovy brochettes

Overall timing 30 minutes

Freezing Not suitable

To serve 2

4	Large slices of white bread	4
4 oz	Mozzarella or Gouda cheese	125 g
3 oz	Butter	75 g
	Salt and pepper	
8	Anchovy fillets	8
4 tbsp	Milk	4 x 15 ml

Preheat the oven to 400°F (200°C) Gas 6.

Cut bread and cheese into small squares. Thread alternately on to four skewers. Arrange in an ovenproof dish so that each end of the skewer is supported by the rim.

Melt half of the butter and brush generously over the brochettes. Season with salt and pepper. Bake for about 15–20 minutes, basting occasionally with butter in dish. The brochettes should be golden brown.

Meanwhile, melt remaining butter in a saucepan. Mash anchovies and add to butter. Gradually add milk and mix well together over gentle heat. Bring to boiling point.

Pour hot anchovy sauce over brochettes and serve immediately.

Prawns magenta

Overall timing 40 minutes

Freezing Not suitable

To serve 2

2	Stalks of celery	2
1	Large carrot	1
1	Small leek	1
2 tbsp	Olive oil	2x15 ml
8 oz	Prawns	225 g
¼ pint	Dry white wine	150 ml
8 oz	Can of tomatoes	225 g
	Salt and pepper	
3	Fresh basil leaves	3
1 oz	Butter	25 g

Trim the celery and cut into thin sticks. Peel the carrot and cut into sticks. Trim and thinly slice the leek.

Heat the oil in a saucepan, add the prepared vegetables, cover and cook over a low heat for 10 minutes to release the flavours without browning vegetables.

Shell the prawns and add to the pan with the white wine and tomatoes and juice. Season, cover and cook over a low heat for 10 minutes, shaking pan occasionally.

Add the whole basil leaves and butter, adjust the seasoning and serve hot with boiled rice.

Prawns ravigote

Overall timing 20 minutes plus marination

Freezing Not suitable

To serve 2

1	Stalk of celery	1
$\frac{1}{2}$	Red pepper	$\frac{1}{2}$
$\frac{1}{2}$	Green pepper	$\frac{1}{2}$
8 oz	Large shelled prawns	225 g
1 teasp	Chopped fresh herbs	5 ml
$\frac{1}{2}$	Round lettuce	$\frac{1}{2}$
1	Hard-boiled egg	1
Marinade		
1 tbsp	Soured cream	15 ml
4 tbsp	Thick mayonnaise	4x15 ml
1 tbsp	Lemon juice	15 ml
1 tbsp	White wine vinegar	15 ml
$\frac{1}{2}$ teasp	Made mustard	2.5 ml
	Salt and pepper	

To make marinade, mix the soured cream and mayonnaise in a bowl. Gradually add the lemon juice and vinegar, a few drops at a time, stirring constantly. Stir in the mustard and season to taste.

Trim the celery and cut into thin strips. Deseed and thinly slice the peppers. Place the prepared vegetables in a bowl and add the chopped prawns and herbs. Pour the marinade over, toss lightly and leave to marinate for 30 minutes.

Wash and dry the lettuce and line serving dish with the leaves. Spoon the prawn salad into the centre.

Shell the egg, cut in half and remove yolk. Slice the white; press yolk through a sieve. Use to garnish the salad.

Prawn omelette in béchamel sauce

Overall timing 40 minutes

Freezing Not suitable

To serve 2

1	Small onion	1
1	Small carrot	1
1	Stalk of celery	1
½ pint	Milk	300 ml
1	Bay leaf	1
2½ oz	Butter	65 g
2 tbsp	Plain flour	2x15 ml
6 oz	Shelled prawns	175 g
2 tbsp	Single cream	2x15 ml
	Salt and pepper	
6	Eggs	6
2 teasp	Chopped parsley	2x5 ml

Peel and roughly chop the onion and carrot. Trim and chop the celery. Put the milk into a saucepan with the bay leaf and prepared vegetables, cover and bring to the boil. Remove from heat and leave to infuse for 10 minutes.

Melt 2 oz (50 g) of the butter in a saucepan, add the flour and cook for 1 minute. Gradually add the strained milk and bring to the boil, stirring constantly. Cook, stirring, for 2 minutes. Reduce heat, stir in prawns, cream and seasoning. Heat without boiling.

Lightly beat the eggs in a bowl with a pinch of salt. Melt remaining butter in a frying pan, pour in the eggs and cook until set.

Spoon half the prawn sauce into the centre of the omelette and fold two sides over. Turn out of pan, placing join side down on warmed serving dish. Pour the remaining sauce round. Make a cut along the top of the omelette to expose the filling, sprinkle the parsley over and serve immediately with a tossed green salad.

Omelette forestière

Overall timing 25 minutes

Freezing Not suitable

To serve 2

4 oz	Thick streaky bacon rashers	125 g
4 oz	Button mushrooms	125 g
2	Small potatoes	2
2 oz	Butter	50 g
4–6	Eggs	4–6
1 tbsp	Chopped parsley	15 ml
	Salt and pepper	

Derind bacon, then cut into thin strips. Thinly slice mushrooms. Peel and thinly slice potatoes. Melt the butter in a frying pan, add potatoes and bacon and fry till tender and golden all over. Add mushrooms and cook for 5 minutes more.

Meanwhile, lightly beat the eggs in a bowl with parsley and seasoning. Pour over the ingredients in the frying pan. Cook for a few minutes, lifting the edges to ensure the underneath is evenly cooked. Fold over and slide on to warmed serving plate. Serve immediately.

Minted cheese omelette

Overall timing 20 minutes

Freezing Not suitable

To serve 2

10	Fresh mint leaves	10
6	Eggs	6
1 oz	Fresh breadcrumbs	25 g
4 oz	Cheese	125 g
	Salt and pepper	
1 tbsp	Chopped parsley	15 ml
1 oz	Butter	25 g

Wash, dry and roughly chop the mint leaves. Lightly beat the eggs in a bowl with the breadcrumbs, grated cheese and seasoning. Stir in the parsley and mint and leave to stand for 5 minutes.

Melt the butter in a frying pan and pour in the egg mixture (or only half if making two omelettes). Tip the pan so that the bottom is coated and cook over a moderate heat until lightly set.

Using a large fish slice, carefully turn the omelette over and cook for 2 minutes more. Serve with tomato salad and wholemeal rolls.

Devilled liver omelettes

Overall timing 20 minutes

Freezing Not suitable

To serve 2

2	Bacon rashers	2
4 oz	Chicken livers	125 g
	Salt and pepper	
1 tbsp	Plain flour	15 ml
2 oz	Mushrooms	50 g
2 oz	Butter	50 g
1 teasp	Tomato purée	5 ml
½ teasp	Worcestershire sauce	2.5 ml
½ teasp	French mustard	2.5 ml
6	Eggs	6
1 teasp	Chopped chives	5 ml

Derind and chop the bacon. Trim and chop the livers and toss in seasoned flour. Slice the mushrooms.

Melt half the butter in a saucepan, add the bacon and fry till light brown. Add the chicken livers and stir-fry till browned. Add the mushrooms, tomato purée, Worcestershire sauce, mustard and seasoning. Mix well, then cover and cook for 3 minutes.

Heat the remaining butter in an omelette pan. Lightly beat the eggs with seasoning and add to pan. Cook until almost set, then spoon the liver mixture over and sprinkle with the chives. Fold omelette, cut in half and place on two warmed plates. Serve hot with granary bread and a tomato and cucumber salad.

Sweet potato soufflé

Overall timing 1¼ hours

Freezing Not suitable

To serve 2

8 oz	Yam or sweet potatoes	225 g
¼ pint	Milk	150 ml
	Salt	
1 oz	Butter	25 g
1½ teasp	Plain flour	7.5 ml
2	Eggs	2
	Pinch of cayenne	
2 oz	Cheese	50 g

Preheat the oven to 375°F (190°C) Gas 5.

Peel the yam or sweet potato and cut into ½ inch (12.5 mm) cubes. Put into a saucepan with the milk and a little salt and bring to the boil. Cover and simmer for about 20 minutes till tender. Drain the yam or sweet potato, reserving the cooking liquor, then return it to the pan and mash over a low heat to make a dry, fluffy purée.

Melt the butter in a saucepan, add the flour and cook for 1 minute. Make the reserved cooking liquor up to ¼ pint (150 ml) with extra milk if necessary and gradually add to the roux. Bring to the boil, stirring constantly, and simmer for 2 minutes. Remove from the heat and allow to cool slightly.

Separate the eggs and beat the yolks into the sauce with the cayenne, grated cheese, a little salt and the yam or potato purée. Whisk the egg whites till stiff and fold into the sauce with a metal spoon.

Pour the mixture into a greased soufflé dish and bake for 30–35 minutes till well risen and golden. Serve immediately.

Avocado soufflé

Overall timing 45 minutes

Freezing Not suitable

To serve 2

1 oz	Butter	25 g
1 oz	Plain flour	25 g
¼ pint	Milk	150 ml
2	Ripe avocados	2
1 teasp	Lemon juice	5 ml
	Pinch of grated nutmeg	
	Salt and pepper	
	Pinch of ground cinnamon *or*	
1 teasp	Grated lemon rind (optional)	5 ml
3	Eggs	3

Preheat the oven to 400°F (200°C) Gas 6.

Melt the butter in a saucepan, stir in the flour and cook for 1 minute. Gradually stir in the milk. Bring to the boil, stirring till thickened. Remove from the heat.

Cut the avocados in half lengthways and lift out the stones. Cut out four very thin slices, sprinkle with lemon juice and reserve for the garnish. Remove remaining flesh with a teaspoon, place it in a bowl and mash well. Add to the sauce and beat vigorously until well blended. Add nutmeg, seasoning and cinnamon or lemon rind, if used.

Separate the eggs. Add the yolks one by one to the saucepan, beating well after each addition. Whisk egg whites with a pinch of salt till very stiff, then gently fold into the sauce.

Pour mixture into a greased 2 pint (1.1 litre) soufflé dish. Place on a baking tray and bake for about 30 minutes till well risen. Garnish with reserved avocado slices and serve immediately.

Spaghetti with goat's cheese

Overall timing 35 minutes

Freezing Not suitable

To serve 2

1	Garlic clove	1
2	Anchovy fillets	2
2 tbsp	Olive oil	2x15 ml
1 tbsp	Chopped parsley	15 ml
	Salt and pepper	
8 oz	Spaghetti	225 g
4 oz	Firm goat's cheese	125 g
1 oz	Butter	25 g

Peel and crush the garlic into a bowl. Add the anchovy fillets and pound to a paste with a wooden spoon. Beat in the oil, parsley and seasoning. Leave to stand for 15 minutes.

Meanwhile, cook the spaghetti in boiling salted water till tender. Derind the cheese and cut into small cubes.

Drain the spaghetti in a colander. Melt the butter in the spaghetti pan and add the cheese. Cook, stirring, over a low heat for 2 minutes.

Return spaghetti to the pan and toss lightly till coated with butter. Arrange in a warmed serving dish, pour the anchovy dressing over and toss lightly before serving with crusty bread.

Neapolitan rigatoni

Overall timing 50 minutes

Freezing Not suitable

To serve 2

2	Streaky bacon rashers	2
1	Onion	1
1	Garlic clove	1
1 oz	Lard	25 g
6 oz	Minced beef	175 g
5 tbsp	Beef stock	5x15 ml
5 tbsp	Red wine	5x15 ml
1 tbsp	Tomato purée	15 ml
1 teasp	Chopped fresh basil	5 ml
	Salt and pepper	
8 oz	Rigatoni	225 g

Derind and finely chop bacon. Peel and chop onion. Peel and crush garlic. Melt the lard in a saucepan, add bacon, onion and garlic and fry for 10 minutes till golden.

Add the minced beef and fry, stirring, till brown. Gradually stir in the stock, wine, tomato purée, basil and seasoning. Cover and simmer for 30 minutes.

Meanwhile, cook rigatoni in boiling salted water till tender. Drain thoroughly and pile on to a warmed serving dish. Keep hot.

Taste the sauce and adjust seasoning. Purée in a blender or press through a sieve, then reheat and spoon over rigatoni. Serve immediately with a mixed salad and grated Parmesan cheese.

Boer-style noodle supper

Overall timing 20 minutes

Freezing Not suitable

To serve 2

1 pint	Milk	560 ml
	Blade of mace	
6 oz	Noodles	175 g
1 oz	Butter	25 g
2	Eggs	2
$\frac{1}{4}$ teasp	Ground cinnamon	1.25 ml
	Salt and pepper	

Put the milk in a saucepan with the mace and bring to the boil. Add the noodles and cook for about 5 minutes till tender. Drain, reserving the milk. Divide noodles between individual soup bowls and add half butter to each. Keep hot.

Separate the eggs. Beat the egg yolks in a bowl with the cinnamon and seasoning. Gradually strain the reserved milk on to the yolks, stirring constantly. Return to the pan.

Whisk the egg whites till stiff and fold into the yolk mixture. Cook over a low heat for 2–5 minutes without stirring till mixture begins to thicken. Do not allow to boil.

Pour egg mixture over the noodles and serve immediately with bread and a mixed salad.

Spinach and veal ravioli

Overall timing 1 hour 35 minutes

Freezing Suitable: cook after thawing

To serve 2

2 oz	Spinach	50 g
6 oz	Veal	175 g
1 oz	Lean cooked ham	25 g
1 oz	Butter	25 g
2 tbsp	Fresh breadcrumbs	2x15 ml
1 tbsp	Milk	15 ml
1	Egg	1
2 oz	Grated Parmesan cheese	50 g
$\frac{1}{4}$ teasp	Dried marjoram	1.25 ml
	Pinch of grated nutmeg	
	Salt and pepper	
12 oz	Ravioli cases	350 g
$\frac{1}{4}$ pint	Tomato sauce	150 ml

Wash spinach and chop roughly. Blanch in boiling water for 5 minutes. Drain.

Chop the veal and ham into small pieces. Melt butter in frying pan and fry veal and ham till brown. Drain and cool. Soak breadcrumbs in milk till milk is absorbed.

Put meats and spinach through a mincer, then mix to a paste. Add egg, soaked breadcrumbs, 2 tbsp (2x15 ml) of the Parmesan, the marjoram, nutmeg and seasoning. Mix together well.

Use mixture to stuff ready-made ravioli cases, which can easily be obtained from delicatessens and supermarkets, then close them up. Cook ravioli in boiling, salted water for about 10 minutes. Drain, place in warmed serving dishes and cover with hot tomato sauce. Sprinkle the ravioli with remaining Parmesan. Serve with a crisp green salad.

Corsican spaghetti

Overall timing 1 hour

Freezing Suitable (sauce only): add olives after reheating

To serve 2

1	Onion	1
2 oz	Butter	50 g
8 oz	Ripe tomatoes	225 g
1	Garlic clove	1
8 oz	Minced beef	225 g
$\frac{1}{2}$	Small dried chilli	$\frac{1}{2}$
	Salt and pepper	
8 oz	Spaghetti	225 g
6	Stoned green olives	6
1 oz	Cheese	25 g

Peel and finely chop onion. Melt half the butter in a saucepan and fry the onion till lightly browned.

Blanch, peel and chop the tomatoes. Peel and crush the garlic and add to onions with the minced beef, tomatoes, the dried chilli and salt. Simmer for 45 minutes.

Cook the spaghetti in boiling salted water till tender. Drain thoroughly in a colander, then add remaining butter and leave to melt.

Remove chilli from sauce. Slice the green olives and add to the sauce. Taste and adjust seasoning.

Pile spaghetti in a warmed serving dish and pour meat sauce over. Serve the grated cheese separately.

Macaroni with artichokes

Overall timing 35 minutes

Freezing Not suitable

To serve 2

2	Small globe artichokes	2
1 teasp	Lemon juice	5 ml
1	Garlic clove	1
2 tbsp	Olive oil	2x15 ml
1 tbsp	Chopped parsley	15 ml
8 oz	Penne macaroni	225 g
	Salt and pepper	

Cut off stems, tough outer leaves and pointed tops of artichokes and snip off the tips of outside leaves. Cut artichokes into quarters, remove chokes and place in bowl with lemon juice. Cover with water and leave to soak for 10 minutes.

Peel and crush garlic. Heat the oil in saucepan. Drain artichokes and add to pan with garlic. Cook gently over low heat for about 10 minutes till tender, turning them several times. Add parsley and cook for a further 5 minutes, stirring occasionally.

Meanwhile, cook macaroni in boiling salted water till tender. Drain thoroughly and add to artichokes. Mix well to coat pasta with oil and parsley, adding lots of seasoning, then turn into warmed serving dish. Serve hot with grated Parmesan cheese.

Pasta with lamb and tomato sauce

Overall timing 1¼ hours

Freezing Not suitable

To serve 2

2	Bacon rashers	2
8 oz	Tomatoes	225 g
1	Onion	1
1	Garlic clove	1
2 tbsp	Oil	2 x 15 ml
6 oz	Minced lamb	175 g
¼ pint	Red wine	150 ml
	Salt and pepper	
8 oz	Pasta shapes	225 g

Derind and chop bacon. Blanch, peel and chop tomatoes. Peel and chop onion and garlic. Heat the oil in a saucepan, add the bacon and fry for 5 minutes. Add onion and garlic and fry gently till transparent. Add the minced lamb and fry for about 15 minutes till browned.

Stir in the red wine, tomatoes and seasoning. Cover and simmer for 40 minutes.

Meanwhile, cook pasta in boiling salted water till tender. Drain and place in warmed serving dish.

Spoon meat sauce over pasta and serve hot with a green salad.

Bean and herring salad

Overall timing 1½ hours

Freezing Not suitable

To serve 2

6 oz	Green beans	175 g
	Salt and pepper	
½ oz	Butter	15 g
2	Matjes herring fillets	2
2	Cooked potatoes	2
1	Onion	1
2 tbsp	Mayonnaise	2 x 15 ml
2 tbsp	Plain yogurt	2 x 15 ml
1 teasp	Lemon juice	5 ml
	Sugar	
	Chopped parsley	

Top and tail the beans and remove strings. Cut into short lengths. Put the beans into a saucepan of boiling salted water, add butter and cook for 10 minutes till just tender. Drain and leave to cool.

Slice the herrings and potatoes. Peel and finely chop the onion. Place in salad bowl and add herrings and potatoes. Lightly mix in beans.

Make the dressing by combining mayonnaise, yogurt, lemon juice and pepper and sugar to taste. Pour over the salad and chill for 1 hour. Serve garnished with chopped parsley.

Courgettes with mozzarella

Overall timing 30 minutes plus chilling

Freezing Suitable: reheat from frozen in 350°F (180°C) Gas 4 oven for 45 minutes

To serve 2

1	Onion	1
1	Garlic clove	1
1 oz	Butter	25 g
3 tbsp	Oil	3x15 ml
8 oz	Can of tomatoes	226 g
¼ teasp	Dried basil	1.25 ml
4	Courgettes	4
2 tbsp	Plain flour	2x15 ml
	Salt and pepper	
4 oz	Mozzarella cheese	125 g

Peel and finely chop onion. Peel and crush garlic. Heat butter and 1 tbsp (15 ml) oil in a frying pan and fry onion and garlic till transparent.

Drain tomatoes. Add to pan with basil and cook over a low heat for 20 minutes. Purée mixture in a blender or push through a sieve.

Trim and slice courgettes. Coat slices with flour. Heat remaining oil in another frying pan and fry courgettes till lightly golden and tender. Drain on kitchen paper and season with salt and pepper.

Thinly slice Mozzarella. Layer courgettes, Mozzarella and tomato sauce in serving dish. Chill for 2–3 hours. Serve with hot garlic bread or toast and butter curls.

Marrow ratatouille

Overall timing 40 minutes

Freezing Suitable: add olives and Parmesan after reheating

To serve 2

1 lb	Marrow	450 g
	Salt and pepper	
1	Onion	1
1	Garlic clove	1
2	Tomatoes	2
1 oz	Butter	25 g
1 tbsp	Oil	15 ml
1 tbsp	Tomato purée	15 ml
5 tbsp	Stock	5x15 ml
1 teasp	Chopped fresh marjoram	5 ml
1 teasp	Chopped fresh basil	5 ml
½ teasp	Chopped fresh thyme	2.5 ml
6	Black olives	6
2 tbsp	Grated Parmesan cheese	2x15 ml

Peel the marrow, cut in half lengthways and scoop out seeds. Cut flesh into 2 inch (5 cm) slices. Blanch in boiling salted water for 5 minutes. Drain well.

Peel and slice the onion. Peel and crush the garlic. Blanch, peel and chop the tomatoes.

Heat butter and oil in a frying pan, add onion and garlic and cook for 5 minutes till transparent. Add marrow, tomatoes, tomato purée, stock, herbs and seasoning. Simmer for 10–15 minutes till the marrow is just tender.

Add the olives and sprinkle with grated Parmesan cheese. Serve hot with chunks of crusty fresh bread, or as an accompaniment to grilled meats.

Roast veal salad

Overall timing 20 minutes

Freezing Not suitable

To serve 2

$\frac{1}{2}$	Round lettuce	$\frac{1}{2}$
$\frac{1}{4}$	Cucumber	$\frac{1}{4}$
2	Large firm tomatoes	2
4	Radishes	4
2	Hard-boiled eggs	2
6 oz	Cold roast veal	175 g
2 tbsp	Oil	2x15 ml
2 teasp	White wine vinegar	2x5 ml
$\frac{1}{2}$ teasp	Powdered mustard	2.5 ml
	Salt and pepper	
	Sprigs of parsley	

Wash and dry lettuce. Use outside leaves to line a serving dish. Shred rest and put in bowl. Cut cucumber into matchsticks and add to shredded lettuce.

Cut tomatoes into wedges. Slice radishes. Add half of each to lettuce and cucumber.

Shell and halve hard-boiled eggs. Cut veal into neat cubes.

Put oil, vinegar, mustard and seasoning into a screw-top jar, cover and shake to mix. Add to shredded lettuce mixture and toss lightly. Place in lettuce-lined dish. Arrange eggs, veal and remaining tomatoes and radishes on top. Garnish with parsley.

Frankfurter kebabs

Overall timing 20 minutes

Freezing Suitable: cook from frozen

To serve 2

4	Frankfurters	4
12	Button onions	12
3 tbsp	Oil	3x15 ml
2 teasp	Coarse-grain mustard	2x5 ml

Preheat the grill.

Cut each frankfurter into three pieces. Blanch onions in boiling water for 5 minutes, then drain and peel. Thread onions and frankfurters alternately on to greased skewers.

Mix oil and mustard together. Brush over kebabs and grill for about 10 minutes, turning and brushing with mustard mixture frequently. Serve with mashed potatoes and pour any cooking juices over.

Chicory bake

Overall timing 45 minutes

Freezing Not suitable

To serve 2

2	Heads of chicory	2
	Salt and pepper	
½ teasp	Sugar	2.5 ml
1 oz	Butter	25 g
½ teasp	Lemon juice	2.5 ml
2	Slices of Gruyère cheese	2
2	Tomatoes	2
	Lettuce leaves	

Place chicory in saucepan of boiling water. Add pinch of salt, sugar, a knob of butter and lemon juice. Cook for 30 minutes.

Preheat the oven to 425°F (220°C) Gas 7.

Drain chicory. Wrap each head in slice of cheese. Place seam-side down in greased ovenproof dish and surround with halved tomatoes. Season well, dot with the rest of the butter and bake for 15 minutes. Garnish with lettuce leaves and serve hot.

Corn prawn salad

Overall timing 15 minutes plus 1 hour chilling

Freezing Not suitable

To serve 2

11½ oz	Can of sweetcorn kernels	326 g
3	Tomatoes	3
8 oz	Shelled prawns	225 g
Dressing		
1	Onion	1
2 tbsp	Herb vinegar	2x15 ml
3 tbsp	Oil	3x15 ml
	Salt and pepper	
1 tbsp	Chopped fresh sage	15 ml
1 tbsp	Chopped parsley	15 ml
1 tbsp	Chopped chives	15 ml

Drain sweetcorn. Blanch and peel tomatoes and cut into strips. Put sweetcorn, tomatoes and prawns in a serving dish.

To make the dressing, peel and finely chop onion. Mix together vinegar, oil and seasoning, then add the onion, sage, parsley and chives.

Pour dressing over salad, mix in well, cover and chill for 1 hour before serving.

Greek salad

Overall timing 40 minutes including chilling

Freezing Not suitable

To serve 2

2	Large tomatoes	2
¼	Cucumber	¼
1	Small onion	1
2 oz	Black olives	50 g
8	Anchovy fillets	8
4 oz	Fetta or Wensleydale cheese	125 g
Dressing		
3 tbsp	Olive oil	3x15 ml
1 tbsp	Lemon juice	15 ml
	Salt and pepper	
	Pinch of dried marjoram	

Quarter tomatoes. Slice cucumber. Peel onion and cut into rings. Stone olives (optional). Roll up anchovy fillets. Cut cheese into chunks. Place all these ingredients in a serving bowl or divide them between two serving dishes.

To make the dressing, mix the oil and lemon juice with pinch of salt, pepper to taste and marjoram. Pour over salad, mix well and chill for 30 minutes before serving.

Another good alternative to Fetta is white Stilton – the important thing is to use a crumbly white cheese with a slightly sour taste. As in the authentic Greek version, it will absorb all the flavour of the oil dressing.

Sunshine salad

Overall timing 15 minutes plus chilling

Freezing Not suitable

To serve 2

8 oz	Poached smoked haddock	225 g
1	Orange	1
1	Grapefruit	1
1	Green pepper	1
1	Onion	1
1 tbsp	Chopped parsley	15 ml
3 tbsp	Olive oil	3x15 ml
1 tbsp	Lemon juice	15 ml
	Salt and pepper	
2 oz	Black olives	50 g

Cut the haddock into small strips. Peel orange and grapefruit and slice or chop the flesh. Deseed and slice pepper. Peel onion and cut into thin rings.

Put prepared ingredients into salad bowl with the parsley. Add oil, lemon juice and seasoning. Toss salad well and chill. Garnish with stoned olives just before serving.

Melon bowl

Overall timing 20 minutes plus chilling

Freezing Not suitable

To serve 2

4 oz	Strawberries	125 g
5 tbsp	Dry white wine	5 x 15 ml
2 tbsp	Granulated sugar	2 x 15 ml
1	Small dessert apple	1
1	Small ripe pear	1
2 oz	Fresh or canned black cherries	50 g
1	Canned pineapple ring	1
1	Small green-skinned honeydew melon	1

Hull the strawberries and purée in a blender with the white wine and sugar. Put into a large bowl.

Peel, core and chop the apple and pear. Halve the cherries and remove stones. Chop the pineapple ring into chunks. Add the prepared fruit to the strawberry purée.

Cut a thin slice from the bottom of the melon so it will stand upright. Cut off the top, scoop out the seeds and discard. Carefully remove the flesh leaving a thick lining in the shell. Cut flesh into neat cubes and add to the other fruit.

Mix well to coat fruit in purée, then pile into the melon shell. Chill for about 2 hours before serving with whipped cream or ice cream.

Melon meringue

Overall timing 25 minutes plus chilling

Freezing Not suitable

To serve 2

1	Ripe ogen melon	1
2 tbsp	Caster sugar	2x15 ml
4 oz	Strawberries or raspberries	125 g
2 tbsp	Grand Marnier	2x15 ml
Meringue		
1	Large egg white	1
2 oz	Caster sugar	50 g

Cut the melon in half horizontally and scoop out the seeds. Sprinkle flesh with caster sugar. Hull strawberries or raspberries and fill the melon cavities with the fruit. Spoon the liqueur over and chill for at least 2 hours.

Preheat the oven to 475°F (240°C) Gas 9.

Whisk egg white till stiff and dry. Fold in the caster sugar. Pipe or spoon the meringue over the melon halves, completely covering the strawberries or raspberries.

Fill a roasting tin with ice cubes and place melon halves in the ice. Bake for about 5 minutes till meringue is lightly browned. Serve immediately in individual dishes containing more ice cubes.

Variations

Use raspberries, blackberries or loganberries to fill the melons. Or fold 1 teasp (5 ml) desiccated coconut into meringue.

Red and black salad

Overall timing 30 minutes plus chilling

Freezing Not suitable

To serve 2

6 oz	Prunes	175 g
1 tbsp	Caster sugar	15 ml
4 tbsp	Water	4x15 ml
2 tbsp	Orange juice	2x15 ml
6 oz	Strawberries	175 g
2 tbsp	Grand Marnier	2x15 ml

Put the prunes into a metal sieve or steamer and place over a saucepan of boiling water. Cover and steam for 15 minutes till plump.

Put the sugar and water into a saucepan and stir over a low heat till the sugar dissolves. Bring to the boil and boil without stirring for 5 minutes. Remove from the heat, stir in the orange juice and leave to cool.

Hull the strawberries. If large, cut them in half lengthways. Slit prunes and carefully remove stones. Arrange prunes and strawberries in two serving dishes.

Add the Grand Marnier to the cold syrup and spoon over the fruit. Leave to macerate in a cool place for 3–4 hours before serving with whipped cream.

Tropical island fruit salad

Overall timing 15 minutes plus maceration

Freezing Not suitable

To serve 2

1	Large orange	1
1	Banana	1
1 tbsp	Lemon juice	15 ml
3	Maraschino cherries	3
1 tbsp	Shelled pistachios	15 ml
5 tbsp	Sweet white wine	5x15 ml
2 tbsp	Curaçao	2x15 ml
1 oz	Caster sugar	25 g
	Vanilla essence	
8 oz	Pawpaw	225 g

Peel the orange, then cut between the membranes with a serrated knife to release the segments. Put into a bowl.

Peel and thinly slice the banana. Sprinkle with 1 teasp (5 ml) of the lemon juice and add to the bowl. Quarter the cherries and add to the bowl with the pistachios. Mix gently.

Pour the white wine, remaining lemon juice and Curaçao over and stir in the sugar and a few drops of vanilla. Leave to macerate for 2 hours in the refrigerator.

Wash the pawpaw. Cut in half lengthways and discard the seeds. Divide fruit salad between the pawpaw halves. Serve immediately on a bed of crushed ice with wafer biscuits or brandy snaps.

Flamed peaches

Overall timing 20 minutes plus chilling

Freezing Not suitable

To serve 2

4 oz	Caster sugar	125 g
½ pint	Water	300 ml
2	Large peaches	2
	Lemon juice	
2 tbsp	Brandy	2 x 15 ml

Dissolve the sugar in the water in a wide saucepan and bring to the boil. Peel, halve and stone the peaches and sprinkle with lemon juice to prevent discoloration. Add the peach halves to the syrup and simmer for 5–10 minutes till translucent. Leave to cool in the syrup.

Just before serving, warm the brandy. Pour it over the peaches, set alight and serve flaming.

Spicy fruit purée

Overall timing 1½ hours plus overnight maceration and cooling

Freezing Suitable

To serve 2

8 oz	Mixed dried fruit (figs, apricots, peaches, pears, prunes)	225 g
1 pint	Water	560 ml
3 oz	Granulated sugar	75 g
1	Apple	1
1 teasp	Ground cinnamon	5 ml
1 tbsp	Cornflour	15 ml

Put the dried fruit in a large bowl with three-quarters of the water and the sugar and leave to soak overnight.

Stone the prunes. Transfer fruit to a saucepan, add remaining water and bring to the boil. Cook over a low heat for about 15 minutes.

Peel, core and slice the apple and add with cinnamon to the pan. Cook for a further 45 minutes.

Drain fruit and return liquid to the pan. Push fruit through a sieve or blend to a purée, then return to the pan.

Mix cornflour with 1 tbsp (15 ml) cold water in a bowl, then stir into fruit mixture. Bring to the boil and boil for 5 minutes, stirring, until thick. Remove from heat and allow to cool. Pour into two serving glasses and chill for 2 hours before serving.

Cherry compôte

Overall timing 2½ hours plus chilling

Freezing Suitable

To serve 2

12 oz	Ripe cherries	350 g
2 oz	Sugar	50 g
1	Small cinnamon stick	1
	Strip of lemon rind	
5 tbsp	Red wine	5 x 15 ml

Remove the stones from the cherries. Place cherries in saucepan with the sugar. Stir gently and leave to macerate for 2 hours.

Add the cinnamon stick, lemon rind and wine and bring to the boil. Simmer for about 15 minutes, till cherries are just tender but not broken. Remove from the heat and allow to cool.

Discard the cinnamon stick and lemon rind and spoon the fruit and liquor into two dishes. Chill for 2 hours before serving.

Fresh fruit fool

Overall timing 30 minutes plus chilling

Freezing Not suitable

To serve 2

8 oz	Mixed fruit (pears, apples, peaches, redcurrants, grapes, cherries)	225 g
5 tbsp	Water	5 x 15 ml
1 oz	Butter	25 g
2 oz	Caster sugar	50 g
1	Large egg yolk	1
4 fl oz	Double cream	120 ml

Cut the pears, apples and peaches into large chunks. Reserve a few redcurrants for the decoration and put the rest of the fruit into a pan with the water. Cook gently until the apples and pears are tender.

Press mixture through a sieve, then return purée to pan. Add the butter, sugar, egg yolk and cream. Heat through gently, stirring. Do not boil.

Transfer to serving bowl, cool slightly then chill. Decorate with redcurrants before serving, with crisp brandy snaps or sponge fingers.

Variations

Replace the water with a sweet white wine and halve the amount of sugar; or add 1 tbsp (15 ml) liqueur to the purée. To give more bulk, stiffly whip the cream instead of adding it to the purée, then whisk the egg white till stiff and fold both into the cooled fruit custard.

Pineapple jelly cream

Overall timing 20 minutes plus chilling

Freezing Suitable

To serve 2

$\frac{1}{2}$	Pineapple jelly tablet	$\frac{1}{2}$
$\frac{1}{4}$ pint	Cold water	150 ml
7 oz	Canned crushed pineapple	200 g
6 tbsp	Whipping cream	6x15 ml
1	Egg white	1

Break up the jelly tablet and put into a small saucepan with half the water. Heat gently, stirring, till the jelly melts, then remove from heat.

Add the crushed pineapple and remaining water, mix well and pour into a large bowl. Chill till beginning to set.

Whip the cream till soft peaks form. Whisk the egg white till stiff but not dry. Fold the cream into the pineapple jelly mixture with a metal spoon, then carefully fold in the egg white.

Pour into two small dishes, smooth the top and chill till lightly set.

Cream cheese and date dessert

Overall timing 25 minutes plus chilling

Freezing Not suitable

To serve 2

3 oz	Dates	75 g
2 tbsp	Benedictine or Drambuie	2x15 ml
6 oz	Cream cheese	175 g
2 tbsp	Single cream	2x15 ml
1 tbsp	Caster sugar	15 ml

Slit the dates open with a sharp knife and remove the stones. Reserve two dates for decoration. Chop the rest and put in a saucepan with the liqueur. Heat gently, stirring with a wooden spoon till dates become mushy. Leave to cool.

Beat together the cream cheese, cream and caster sugar in a bowl till fluffy. Stir in cooked dates. Spoon mixture into piping bag. Pipe into two serving glasses. Decorate with the reserved whole dates and chill for 30 minutes before serving.

Strawberry cheese desserts

Overall timing 15 minutes plus chilling

Freezing Not suitable

To serve 2

6 oz	Cream cheese	175 g
1 tbsp	Milk	15 ml
1 tbsp	Single cream	15 ml
1½ tbsp	Caster sugar	22.5 ml
¼ teasp	Vanilla essence	1.25 ml
2½ tbsp	Redcurrant jelly	37.5 ml
1 tbsp	Cointreau or Curaçao	15 ml
4 oz	Strawberries	125 g

Beat the cream cheese with the milk, cream, 1 tbsp (15 ml) of the sugar and the vanilla. Divide mixture between two serving glasses and chill for 1 hour.

Melt the redcurrant jelly and remaining sugar in a saucepan, add Cointreau or Curaçao and allow to cool.

Hull strawberries and divide between glasses. Spoon the redcurrant mixture over the strawberries, then serve immediately with crisp biscuits.

Mont Blanc

Overall timing 1¼ hours plus 1 hour chilling

Freezing Not suitable

To serve 2

8 oz	Chestnuts	225 g
1½ oz	Plain dessert chocolate	40 g
1 tbsp	Rum	15 ml
2 oz	Icing sugar	50 g
¼ pint	Carton of double cream	150 ml
	Crystallized violets	

Using a sharp knife, score chestnuts from base to top point. Cook in boiling water for 40 minutes.

Drain chestnuts. Cool under cold running water. Remove shells and skin. Press through sieve or purée in a food mill.

Break chocolate into pieces and melt in a bowl placed over a pan of hot water. Remove from heat and allow to cool.

Add chestnut purée, rum and icing sugar to cooled chocolate and mix together well. Press through a large-holed sieve so mixture resembles spaghetti. Pile into a mountain shape on serving dish.

Whip cream and spoon over chestnut mixture. Decorate with crystallized violets. Chill for 1 hour before serving.

Chocolate liqueur mousse

Overall timing 45 minutes plus chilling

Freezing Not suitable

To serve 2

4 oz	Plain dessert chocolate	125 g
½ oz	Butter	15 g
1 tbsp	Water	15 ml
1 tbsp	Tia Maria	15 ml
5 tbsp	Double cream	5x15 ml
1	Egg	1
2 teasp	Caster sugar	2x5 ml

Break the chocolate into pieces and put into a bowl over a saucepan of hot water. Add the butter, water and Tia Maria and stir over gentle heat till melted and smooth. Allow to cool.

Whip the cream till soft peaks form. Separate egg. Place egg yolk and sugar in a bowl and whisk over hot water till frothy. Cool.

Gently stir the chocolate mixture into the whisked egg yolk. Fold the whipped cream into chocolate mixture. Whisk the egg white till stiff but not dry. Fold into the chocolate mixture. Chill for 4 hours before serving.

Blackberry pancakes

Overall timing 30 minutes

Freezing Not suitable

To serve 2

1½ oz	Plain flour	40 g
2 teasp	Caster sugar	2x5 ml
	Pinch of salt	
1	Egg	1
3 fl oz	Milk	90 ml
	Oil for frying	
Topping		
4 oz	Canned blackberries	125 g
3 tbsp	Honey	3x15 ml
1½ tbsp	Brandy	22.5 ml
	Vanilla ice cream	
1 oz	Walnuts	25 g

Sift flour, sugar and salt into a bowl. Make a well in the centre and add egg and milk. Whisk till smooth. Pour into jug and leave to stand for 5 minutes.

Lightly oil an 8 inch (20 cm) pancake pan and heat. Make four thin pancakes. Fold into quarters, arrange on a warmed serving plate and keep hot.

Place drained blackberries in a sieve and rinse under running water. Turn on to kitchen paper to drain.

Gently heat honey with brandy in a saucepan. Remove from heat before it boils.

To assemble pancakes, put a cube of ice cream on top of each and scatter with blackberries. Pour over hot honey mixture and sprinkle with chopped walnuts. Serve immediately.

Fruity pancakes

Overall timing 1 hour

Freezing Not suitable

To serve 2

1½ oz	Plain flour	40 g
2 teasp	Caster sugar	2x5 ml
	Pinch of salt	
1	Egg	1
4 tbsp	Milk	4x15 ml
2 tbsp	Cider or white wine	2x15 ml
	Grated **rind of** ½ orange	
	Vanilla essence	
3	Sugar lumps	3
1	Orange	1
½ teasp	Ground cinnamon	2.5 ml
2	Dessert apples	2
	Oil for frying	

Sift flour, sugar and salt into a bowl. Make a well in the centre and add egg, milk, cider or wine, orange rind and a few drops of vanilla essence. Whisk till smooth. Pour batter into a jug.

Rub sugar lumps over surface of orange to absorb zest. Crush them and add cinnamon.

Peel orange, then chop flesh roughly. Place in a bowl. Peel, core and cube apples, then mix well with orange.

Preheat the grill.

Lightly oil an 8 inch (20 cm) pancake pan and heat. Pour in one-quarter of the batter and cook for 1–2 minutes till base bubbles and is firm. Spoon over one-quarter of the fruit and crushed sugar and cinnamon mixtures. Place under grill and cook for a few minutes till bubbling. Fold pancake and lift out on to a warmed serving dish. Cover and keep hot while you cook three other pancakes in the same way.

Serve whipped cream flavoured with orange juice separately, or serve with vanilla ice cream.

Jam omelettes

Overall timing 10 minutes

Freezing Not suitable

To serve 2

3	Eggs	3
	Pinch of salt	
1 oz	Butter	25 g
3 tbsp	Jam	3x15 ml
1 tbsp	Caster sugar	15 ml

Beat eggs with salt in a bowl. Melt half butter in omelette pan. Add half the egg mixture and cook until set. Slip omelette out of pan on to plate, cooked side down.

Repeat with remaining egg mixture to make another omelette. Spoon jam into the middle of each omelette. Roll them up like pancakes and sprinkle with caster sugar.

To make the caramelized stripes, heat a skewer or toasting fork over a naked flame, then press lightly on top of the omelettes at intervals. Serve at once.

Apple soufflé omelette

Overall timing 50 minutes

Freezing Not suitable

To serve 2

2	Eggs	2
2 tbsp	Caster sugar	2x15 ml
4 tbsp	Milk	4x15 ml
¼ teasp	Vanilla essence	1.25 ml
1 oz	Butter	25 g
	Icing sugar	
2 tbsp	Brandy	2x15 ml
Filling		
12 oz	Cooking apple	350 g
1 tbsp	Water	15 ml
½ oz	Butter	15 g
3 tbsp	Granulated sugar	3x15 ml
	Vanilla essence	

To make the filling, peel, core and roughly chop apple. Place in saucepan with water and butter, cover and cook for 15 minutes. Remove from heat and add sugar and few drops of vanilla essence. Mix well, then cool.

To make omelette, separate one egg. Put the yolk in a bowl with the whole egg and the caster sugar and beat till light and frothy. Stir in milk and vanilla essence.

In another bowl, beat the egg white till very stiff. Stir 1 tbsp (15 ml) into yolk mixture to lighten it, then carefully fold in the rest with a metal spoon.

Preheat the grill.

Melt the butter in an omelette pan. When it begins to turn a light brown, pour in the egg mixture. Cook over a low heat for 5–7 minutes. Place under the grill until the top has set. Spread over the filling and fold over in half. Slide onto a warmed serving dish. Dredge with icing sugar. Warm the brandy, pour over the omelette and set alight. Serve flaming.

Banana soufflés

Overall timing 25 minutes

Freezing Not suitable

To serve 2

4	Ripe bananas	4
1 oz	Butter	25 g
3 oz	Caster sugar	75 g
	Vanilla essence	
2 tbsp	Rum	2x15 ml
2	Large eggs	2
2 tbsp	Icing sugar	2x15 ml

Preheat the oven to 425°F (220°C) Gas 7.

Make two lengthways slits with a sharp knife near to the top of each banana, leaving the skin joined at the stalk end. Roll back skin. Remove banana pulp with a teaspoon and place in a bowl. Mash well to a purée.

Put the banana purée into a saucepan with the butter, caster sugar, a few drops of vanilla essence and the rum. Cook for about 3 minutes over a low heat, stirring constantly. Remove from heat.

Separate eggs. Stir yolks into the banana mixture. Place pan in cold water to cool mixture quickly. Beat egg whites till firm, then lightly fold into cold banana mixture with a metal spoon.

Fill banana skins with mixture. Place on a baking tray and bake for about 10 minutes. Sprinkle with icing sugar and serve immediately with pouring cream.

Banana split

Overall timing 30 minutes

Freezing Not suitable

To serve 2

4 oz	Strawberries	125 g
2 oz	Grapes	50 g
1	Small orange	1
1	Kiwi fruit	1
1 teasp	Arrowroot	5 ml
2 tbsp	Milk shake syrup	2x15 ml
5 tbsp	Double cream	5x15 ml
2	Bananas	2
	Vanilla ice cream	
4	Little meringues	4

Hull strawberries and cut them in half. Halve grapes and remove pips. Peel orange (be careful to remove pith) and divide into segments. Peel and slice kiwi fruit. Place all the fruits in a bowl, and chill for 15 minutes.

Mix arrowroot with a little hot water and blend into milk shake syrup to thicken it. Whip cream to piping consistency.

Peel bananas. "Split" in half lengthways and place halves down each side of two serving dishes. Arrange fruit between bananas and place scoops of ice cream on top. Pour over a little syrup, pipe on cream swirls and top with meringues. Serve immediately with crisp fan wafers.

Iced grape dessert

Overall timing 20 minutes plus freezing

Freezing See method

To serve 2

10 oz	Black grapes	275 g
1 tbsp	Lemon juice	15 ml
3 tbsp	Dry white wine	3x15 ml
1 teasp	Maraschino	5 ml
5 tbsp	Cane or golden syrup	5x15 ml

Wash grapes and remove from stem. Put into a pan with the lemon juice, wine and Maraschino. Bring to the boil and simmer gently for 5 minutes till soft.

Remove from heat and press through a sieve into a bowl. Allow to cool slightly, then stir in the syrup.

Turn mixture into freezer tray. Leave to cool completely, then place in freezer and freeze till firm. Scoop into individual glasses and serve with crisp almond biscuits.

Peach sundae

Overall timing 40 minutes plus maceration

Freezing Not suitable

To serve 2

2	Large ripe peaches	2
1 tbsp	Maraschino or peach brandy	15 ml
1½ oz	Caster sugar	40 g
1 tbsp	Apricot jam	15 ml
	Peach or vanilla ice cream	

Peel, halve and stone one of the peaches. Roughly chop the flesh and put into a bowl with the Maraschino or peach brandy and sugar. Macerate in the refrigerator for 30 minutes.

In a saucepan, melt the apricot jam with 1 tbsp (15 ml) of macerating liquid. Peel, halve and stone remaining peach. Divide chopped fruit and juices between two serving dishes and top each with cubes of ice cream and a peach half. Spoon the warmed jam over and serve immediately.

Redcurrant coupe

Overall timing 25 minutes

Freezing Not suitable

To serve 2

4 oz	Redcurrants	125 g
½ oz	Split almonds	15 g
4 fl oz	Double cream	120 ml
	Vanilla essence	
2 teasp	Caster sugar	2x5 ml
	Vanilla ice cream	

Wash and drain the redcurrants. Remove the stalks. Coarsely chop the almonds.

Whip the cream with a few drops of vanilla essence and the sugar till stiff. Put into a piping bag fitted with a star nozzle.

Reserve a few of the redcurrants, then divide the rest between two chilled glasses. Top with cubes of ice cream and sprinkle with chopped almonds. Pipe swirls of the cream on top and decorate with reserved redcurrants. Serve immediately with wafers.

Bilberries with cream

Overall timing 30 minutes

Freezing Not suitable

To serve 2

8 oz	Fresh or frozen bilberries	225 g
3 oz	Caster sugar	75 g
1 oz	Flaked almonds	25 g
$\frac{1}{4}$ pint	Carton of double cream	150 ml
3 oz	Cream cheese	75 g
1 tbsp	Cointreau *or*	15 ml
2 tbsp	Orange juice	2x15 ml

Thaw frozen bilberries. Sprinkle with half the caster sugar.

Preheat the grill.

Spread flaked almonds on grill pan and toast until brown.

Whip cream with 1 teasp (5 ml) of the remaining caster sugar. In another bowl, beat cream cheese with rest of caster sugar and the Cointreau or orange juice.

Mix the cream mixture into the cheese mixture. Spoon a little into each of two glasses, then top with bilberries. Put remaining cream/ cheese mixture into piping bag and swirl some on to each glass. Decorate with toasted almonds and serve immediately.

Cherry snowballs

Overall timing 45 minutes plus chilling

Freezing Not suitable

To serve 2

7 fl oz	Milk	200 ml
$\frac{1}{2}$ oz	Butter	15 g
3 oz	Sugar	75 g
2 oz	Pudding rice	50 g
2 teasp	Powdered gelatine	2x5 ml
4 tbsp	Double cream	4x15 ml
	Vanilla essence	
2 oz	Chopped almonds	50 g
1 tbsp	Cherry brandy	15 ml
8 oz	Can of red cherries	225 g
1 teasp	Arrowroot	5 ml
	Almond essence	

Bring milk, butter, 2 oz (50 g) sugar and pinch of salt to the boil in a saucepan. Stir in rice and simmer gently for 30 minutes.

Meanwhile, dissolve gelatine in 1 tbsp (15 ml) water. Whip cream till thick. Add gelatine and cream to rice mixture with few drops of vanilla essence, the almonds and cherry brandy. Spoon into dampened moulds and chill till set.

Drain cherries, reserving 5 tbsp (5x15 ml) juice and mix this with arrowroot. Add remaining sugar and few drops of almond essence. Bring to the boil and cook until thickened. Add cherries and cool.

Turn out rice moulds and serve with cherry sauce.

Strawberry sundae

Overall timing 20 minutes

Freezing Not suitable

To serve 2

6 oz	Strawberries	175 g
1 tbsp	Strawberry jam	15 ml
1 tbsp	Kirsch	15 ml
6 tbsp	Double cream	6x15 ml
	Almond essence	
	Vanilla ice cream	

Hull the strawberries. Reserve six firm ones and press the rest through a nylon sieve into a pan. Add the jam and Kirsch, and stir over a gentle heat till smooth. Rub through a sieve into two serving glasses. Leave to cool.

Meanwhile, whip the cream till stiff peaks form. Fold in few drops of almond essence.

Top the strawberry purée with a scoop of ice cream and a swirl of cream and decorate with the reserved strawberries. Serve immediately with crisp biscuits.

Variations

Replace the almond essence with $\frac{1}{2}$ oz (15 g) toasted nuts, or use chocolate dots and serve with chocolate ice cream.

Cinnamon creams

Overall timing 1 hour plus chilling time

Freezing Suitable: decorate with cream after thawing

To serve 2

$\frac{1}{4}$ pint	Milk	150 ml
1	Small cinnamon stick	1
4 fl oz	Double cream	120 ml
2	Small eggs	2
$1\frac{1}{2}$ oz	Caster sugar	40 g
1 teasp	Ground cinnamon	5 ml
1 teasp	Powdered gelatine	5 ml
1 tbsp	Water	15 ml
2 teasp	Icing sugar	2x5 ml

Put milk and cinnamon stick into a saucepan and bring to the boil. Remove from heat and leave to infuse. Remove cinnamon stick from milk. Stir in half cream.

Separate eggs. Beat yolks with caster sugar and half ground cinnamon till thick and creamy. Add to milk and cream mixture and cook gently for 10–15 minutes, stirring till thick. Remove from heat and cool.

Dissolve gelatine in water and stir into cream mixture. Leave till thickened. Whisk egg whites with a pinch of salt till soft peaks form. Fold into cream mixture. Divide between serving dishes and chill for 1 hour.

Whip remaining cream with icing sugar and pipe on top of cream mixture. Sprinkle with remaining ground cinnamon and serve.

Index